OUR PLACES OF WORSHIP

Buddhism

Honor Head

WAYLAND

First published in 2009
by Wayland

Copyright © Wayland 2009

Wayland
338 Euston Road
London NW1 3BH

Wayland Australia
Level 17/207 Kent Street
Sydney NSW 2000

Commissioning editor: Jennifer Sanderson
Editor: Jean Coppendale
Designer: Alix Wood
Consultant: Imogene Majsai, B.Ed, teacher at the
    Dharma Buddhist School, Brighton, England

British Library Cataloguing in Publication Data
Head, Honor.
    Buddhism. – (Our places of worship)
    1. Temples, Buddhist–Juvenile literature.
    2. Public worship – Buddhism – Juvenile literature.
    3. Buddhism – Juvenile literature.
    I. Title II. Series 294.3'435-dc22

ISBN 978 0 7502 4930 0

This book can be used in conjunction with the interactive CD-Rom, *Our Places of Worship*. To do this, look for ⊙ and the file path. For example, Buddhist temples can be found on Buddhism/Temples/Buddhist temples. From the whiteboard, click on 'Buddhism', 'Temples' and then 'Buddhist temples'.

sample from the CD-Rom, log on to www.waylandbooks.co.uk.

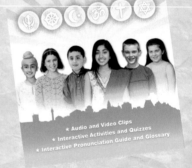

Our Places of Worship
Single user licence: ISBN 978 0 7502 5303 1
School library service licence: ISBN 978 0 7502 5532 5
Site user licence ISBN 978 0 7502 5533 2

Picture credits:
l = left r = right m = middle t = top b= bottom
Cover, 5, 7, 8t, 9l, 10, 11, 12, 13 Discovery Media/Our Places of Worship; 6 Mervyn Rees/Alamy; 8b Asia/Alamy; 9r age fotostock/Superstock; 14 Marilyn Barbone/Shutterstock; 15 Ilse Schrama/Alamy; 16 Robert Paulvan Beets/Shutterstock; 17 Pep Roig/Alamy; 18 Danita Delimont/Alamy; 19 Edward Karaa/Alamy; 20 PatitucciPhoto/Getty Images; 21 Maciej Wojtkowiak/Ark Religion; 22 imagebroker/Alamy; 23t Sherab/Alamy; 23m 2265524729/Shutterstock; 23b Julien Grondin/Shutterstock; 24 World Religions Photo Library/Alamy; 25 Andrew Woodley/Alamy; 26 Frans Lemmens/Alamy; 27 Pep Roig/Alamy; 28 Photosindia.com RM Batch 7/Alamy; 28 Dinodia Photo Library/Ark Religions

Printed in China

Wayland is a division of Hachette Children's Books,
an Hachette UK company.
www.hachette.co.uk

Contents

Words appearing in
bold, like this, can be
found in the glossary
on page 30.

What is a temple?

Buddhists can meet and **meditate** anywhere, but many like to meet in special **temples** or centres. Buddhist temples are sometimes called viharas. Each temple has a statue or image of the Buddha, the founder of Buddhism. Worshippers can visit the temple at any time or day. Most Buddhist temples are specially built, but some are ordinary houses that have been made into temples. Usually Buddhist temples are very bright and colourful.

▶ The Buddhapadipa temple in Wimbledon, London, was the first Buddhist temple in the United Kingdom. It was opened in 1976.

⊙ Buddhism/Temples/Buddhist Temples

▲ The Birmingham Buddhist Centre, England was once a house. It was then used as a synagogue (a Jewish place of worship) before it became a Buddhist centre in 1996.

Monks and nuns

Buddhist **monks** and **nuns** look after the temples. They often live, eat and sleep there, too. The monks and nuns keep the **shrine** clean and tidy, and spend their time studying the works of the Buddha and meditating. They are an important part of the Buddhist community and help others who are interested in learning about Buddhism.

WHAT DO YOU THINK?

Why do you think Buddhists have a statue of the Buddha in their temples?

Why do you think it is important to have a special place in which to worship?

Welcome to the temple

Buddhists visit their local temple to pay their respects to the Buddha. This is called **puja**. Worshippers take off their shoes before they go into the temple. This shows respect for the temple. It also shows that the person is leaving everyday problems and thoughts outside the temple and is concentrating on the Buddha and his teachings.

Shrine room

The main part of the temple is the shrine room, which contains a statue of the Buddha. This statue is called the Buddha rupa and it is the most important part of the shrine room. People put their hands together and bow in front of the Buddha rupa. This shows how important Buddha is and how his teachings make a difference to the lives of all Buddhists.

▶ Worshippers kneel and bow to the Buddha rupa when they enter the shrine room.

6

▼ The shrine in the shrine room is the most important part of the Buddhist temple. It contains many objects including a **stupa**, **incense** and a golden statue of the Buddha.

shrine

Buddha rupa

candles

incense

stupa

flowers

Flowers and candles

Many people take fresh flowers to the shrine every day. The flowers remind Buddhists that nothing lasts for ever. The flowers are beautiful now, but will soon wither and die. Buddhists also light candles to remember how the Buddha's teachings light up the world.

Incense

Buddhists keep sticks of incense on the shrine because they have a sweet smell. This reminds worshippers of the sweetness of the Buddha's teachings and how they have spread around the world.

▲ Incense sticks are lit on the shrine. Flowers remind Buddhists that everything changes.

▲ This worshipper is leaving an offering at a Buddhist shrine in a street in Bangkok, Thailand.

STREET SHRINES

In many countries, such as India and Thailand, there are shrines in the street with statues of the Buddha. People leave offerings of food and flowers. During festivals and holy days, Buddhists clean the statues and decorate them with flowers and incense.

⊙ Buddhism/Temples/The Shrine Room

The stupa

Sometimes there is a model of a stupa on the shrine. Stupas are **sacred** buildings or **burial mounds** that are common in Asia. They are shaped like a dome. Buddhists walk around the stupas in a clockwise direction, often **chanting** as they walk. In the shrine room, special items are kept in the model of the stupa, such as sacred writings.

THE FIRST STUPA

The stupa at Sarnath in India, is built on the place where the Buddha gave the first teachings about his beliefs. The five **holy men** who gathered to listen to him were his first followers. They then went out and spread the Buddha's teachings to others.

▲ The stupa at Sarnath, near the city of Varanasi in northern India.

◄ All models of the stupa are usually the same shape. The round mound reminds Buddhists of air, earth, fire and water. The pointed spire stands for wisdom and learning.

Puja in the temple

At the start of puja, Buddhists make offerings of flowers, incense and food to the statue of the Buddha. Buddhists do not pray to the Buddha but they show that they respect him and his teachings. Buddhists try to follow the Buddha's good example.

Songs and blessings

During puja, people sit on the floor with their legs crossed or kneeling. They chant stanzas (verses) that are special blessings that they repeat over and over again. This is a way for worshippers to show their belief in the teachings of the Buddha with their voice, body and mind.

▼ Worshippers offer flowers and food to the Buddha. They also light candles.

⊙ Buddhism/Worship/Puja in the Temple

Love and kindness

During puja, worshippers remember what it is the Buddha wants of them. The Buddha taught that people should be kind and give to those who are poor. Buddhists believe that nothing living should be harmed.

The holy thread

As part of puja, the monks chant blessings over the holy thread, which is an orange piece of string. In some temples the string is a different colour. Usually the string is attached to the Buddha rupa and wound around the wrist of everyone in the room and then back to the statue. This is to show that everyone is united in their love for the Buddha. At the end of the chanting, the string is unwound. Then the monks tie a piece of the string around every person's wrist so that they can carry the blessings with them.

▲ During puja, the holy thread is wound around everyone's wrist, joining them all together.

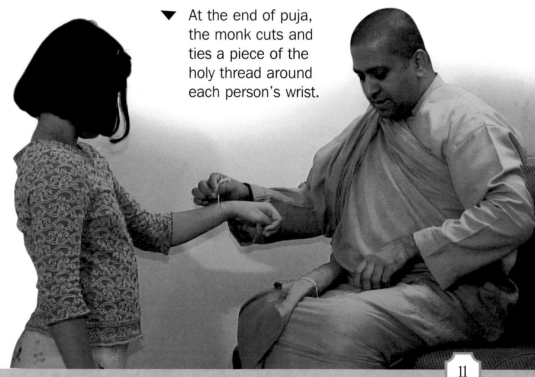

▼ At the end of puja, the monk cuts and ties a piece of the holy thread around each person's wrist.

The Triple Gem

As part of puja everyone says a verse. The verse may be about the Triple Gem, the three main Buddhist beliefs. These are sometimes called the Three Jewels because they are so precious.

The three parts of the Triple Gem are:
1. Belief in the Buddha;
2. Belief in the Dharma — the Buddha's teachings;
3. Belief in the Sangha — the Buddhist monks and nuns and anyone who believes in the teachings of the Buddha.

MONKS AND NUNS

Buddhist monks and nuns are people who have chosen to live their life following the teachings of the Buddha. They also teach others about Buddhism and give advice and help to people in the local community.

▲ Buddhist monks and nuns spend a lot of their time studying the works of the Buddha and meditating.

▲ During puja, worshippers chant some of the Buddha's teachings.

⦿ Buddhism/Worship/Puja in the Temple

Being calm

At the end of puja everyone meditates for a while. Meditation is a very important part of Buddhist beliefs (see pages 14-15). During meditation people sit quietly and breathe slowly. This helps them to become calm and happy and feel good about life. After puja, everyone goes into another room and shares food that has been made by helpers at the temple.

▼ During meditation, everyone sits quietly with their eyes shut.

Meditation

For many Buddhists meditation is an important part of learning to calm the mind. By sitting quietly they can concentrate on the teachings of the Buddha. Meditation helps to clear their minds of everyday thoughts and clutter. When Buddhists meditate at the temple they sit cross-legged on the floor and close their eyes. They breathe slowly and count their breaths in and out for a minute or two. Then they think about doing something that they really enjoy with friends or family. They could also think about how they can help people they know.

▶ The Buddha spent a lot of time meditating to help him to find the path to true happiness.

⊙ Buddhism/Worship/Meditation

Meditating anywhere

Most Buddhists sit on the floor to meditate, but they can sit anywhere in a quiet place. They can meditate under a tree in the park, or at home in a chair. Some people meditate by imagining that they can see a candle flame flickering, some by breathing slowly and deeply.

Walking meditation

Some Buddhists practise a form of walking meditation. They walk slowly somewhere quiet, such as in a park, on a beach or in a wood. They think about how their body feels as it moves. They concentrate on the present moment and try not worry about the past or the future.

▲ Buddhist monks follow the Buddha's teachings and meditate as much as they can.

WHAT DO YOU THINK?

Try to meditate for three minutes. Did you think it was easy or hard?

Why do you think meditation helps to keep you calm and feel more relaxed?

⊙ Buddhism/Worship/Meditation

The Buddha

The Buddha's name was Siddhartha Gautama. He was born in India in the 5th century BCE. Siddhartha was a prince and he was rich and powerful. His father built him four palaces and Siddhartha lived in each one, moving from one beautiful home to another.

Seeing suffering

When he was 28 years old, Siddhartha left the palace grounds. In the outside world he saw a funeral, a sick man and an old man. For the first time in his life, he saw people suffering. He was very upset by what he saw and decided to try and do something about it.

◀ This statue of the Buddha holds an empty pot. This stands for a person who is empty and waiting to be filled with the teachings of the Buddha.

Shaved head and robes

Siddhartha shaved his head and changed his grand clothes for simple robes. He spent many years travelling around India, speaking with holy men, trying to discover why people suffered. Then one day, he saw a great **Bodhi tree**, the 'tree of wisdom'. He sat under the tree for a long time and meditated.

Enlightenment

Stories tell that on a night of the full moon, Siddhartha gained **Enlightenment**. This means he understood the meaning of life and why people suffered. From this time, Siddhartha was known as the Buddha, which means 'Awakened One'. For the rest of his life, the Buddha taught others how to live to find true happiness and Enlightenment.

THE BODHI TREE

A Bodhi tree is a type of fig tree. Buddhists often tie a prayer flag to a Bodhi tree. A prayer flag a cloth with a prayer written on it. When the wind moves the cloth, the prayer flies into the air.

The Buddha's teachings

The Buddha believed that people suffer because of the way they live and treat each other. He taught that people can be greedy and selfish. He explained that unhappiness is caused because people want things they do not have and are always looking for bigger and better things. Buddhist monks and nuns have very few possessions. They own only the robes that they wear, a razor to shave their heads and a bowl in which to collect food.

▼ Buddhist monks do not have any money to buy food. Instead, local people give them rice and vegetables each day.

Dharmachakra

The Buddha said that if people follow the Dharmachakra (also called the **Dharma Wheel** or Eightfold Path), they will be happier. The Eightfold Path shows Buddhists how to think, speak and act in the right way. The Dharmachakra has eight spokes, or paths. Each path shows a way for Buddhists to be happy by understanding life, doing good things and keeping their minds peaceful.

▼ The Dharmachakra is often used as a symbol for the Buddha's teachings.

Right meditation

Right effort

Right attitude

Right thoughts

Right understanding

Right work

Right action

Right speech

Five choices

Buddhists believe that there five choices that can help them to make their lives better. These are:

1. Not to hurt any living thing;
2. Not to steal, and to be generous;
3. Not to be greedy, and to share;
4. Not to lie or say unkind things;
5. Not to drink alcohol or use drugs. When people are drunk or on drugs, they cannot think clearly or make good choices.

▼ Buddhist monks share what little they have and often look after stray cats and dogs.

Perfect peace

The Buddha taught that there is a cycle of birth, life and death and rebirth. This cycle happens again and again until you find perfect peace and do not suffer any more. This perfect peace is called **Nirvana**. Buddhists try to reach Nirvana by following the Buddha's teachings and by meditating.

Holy writings

All of the Buddha's teachings are written in a book called the Tipitaka. The book is written in an ancient Indian language called Pali. The Tipitaka has three sections that are known as the 'three baskets of wisdom'. These teach people how to live good lives that follow the Buddha's teachings. The holy book also describes the experiences of the Buddha and explains his teachings.

WHAT DO YOU THINK?

Why do you think wanting bigger and better things could make people unhappy?

What would be the most difficult part of the Buddha's teachings to follow?

▶ This monk is making an offering to the Buddha. Monks spend their life following the teachings of the Buddha and trying to reach Enlightenment.

Signs and symbols

Some of the teachings of the Buddha can be hard to understand. Using signs and symbols to explain these beliefs helps to make them clear to everyone. Using signs and symbols instead of words also means that different ideas can be explained to people who cannot read the original language of the Buddha's teachings.

▶ This Buddhist temple in Vietnam is decorated with a statue of the Buddha and lotus flowers. This helps visitors to recognise the temple as a Buddhist centre.

Wheel of life

The Dharma Wheel (see page 19) helps people to understand the teachings of the Buddha. The eight spokes, or paths, remind people of the eight ways to lead a good life. The sign of the wheel is often used for decoration, especially on Buddhist temples.

▼ The Dharma Wheel on top of this building tells people that it is a Buddhist temple.

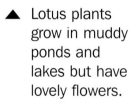

Lotus flowers

The beautiful lotus flower has its roots in muddy water but it grows towards the sunlight. Lotus flowers are a symbol of the Buddhist belief that people can change and grow towards Enlightenment and Nirvana.

▲ Lotus plants grow in muddy ponds and lakes but have lovely flowers.

▲ The head, hair and ears of the Buddha statue have special meanings.

SYMBOLS OF THE BUDDHA

Statues of the Buddha have lots of symbols. In this statue, the bump on the Buddha's head shows that he is a special person. His long earlobes mean he came from an important family. The Buddha's curly hair is a symbol of holiness.

Buddhist festivals

There are many festivals when Buddhists visit their temples and make offerings to statues of the Buddha.

Buddha Day

Wesak, or Buddha Day, is one the most important festivals. This is the day when Buddhists celebrate the birthday of Siddhartha, his Enlightenment, and the day he passed away. Buddhists believe these things happened on the same day but many years apart.

▼ A Buddhist monk blesses worshippers on Wesak Day in Malaysia.

Special celebrations

On Buddha Day, Buddhists decorate their temples with flowers and streamers. They also wash the statue of the Buddha. In some parts of the world, such as India, there are parades. At night, worshippers walk around a statue of the Buddha with candles or lamps to remember the light his teachings have given them.

Floating boats

In some parts of the world, especially in Thailand, the Buddhist festival of Loy Krathong is very important. People make small boats from paper or palm leaves. As the moon rises they put a lit candle, flowers and incense in the boat and set it afloat. It is good luck if the candle stays burning until the boat is out of sight. The candle represents the Buddha and the boat symbolises letting go of all bad thoughts and actions.

THE BUDDHA'S TOOTH

In Sri Lanka, Buddhists celebrate Perahera or the festival of the Buddha's Sacred Tooth. It is believed that a tooth from the Buddha was found in his ashes when his body was **cremated**. The tooth is kept in a special place, but on the last day of Perahera it is carried through the streets on the back of an elephant.

▲ These boys are sailing their boats to celebrate Loy Krathong in Thailand.

Holy places

There are many places that have an important meaning for Buddhists. Most of these are in India where the Buddha travelled, gained Enlightenment and passed away. Many Buddhists visit these places as a sign of respect to the Buddha. They also go there to help themselves on their own journey to Enlightenment.

Lumbini

At Lumbini in Nepal, South Asia, there is a pool where Buddhists believe Siddhartha's mother bathed just before giving birth to her son. Many Buddhists make **pilgrimages** to Lumbini to pay their respects to the Buddha.

◀ This statue of the Buddha as a baby is in a temple built near the sacred pool at Lumbini.

Bodhi tree

One of the holiest places for Buddhists to visit is in Bodh Gaya, near Patna in India. Buddhists believe that this was where the Buddha found Enlightenment. A Bodhi tree grows on the exact spot where the Buddha sat as he meditated. Near the tree is a stone that the Buddha sat on, and carvings of his footprints.

Pilgrims

Buddhists from all over the world go to the Bodh Gaya to meet and talk about the teachings of the Buddha. Many just come here as a sign of their love for him. **Pilgrims** leave flowers for the Buddha and light candles and incense. Some Buddhists also meditate under the tree.

▶ Buddhists meet under the Bodhi tree where they believe that the Buddha became Enlightened. The tree is covered in colourful prayer flags.

⊙ Buddhism/Signs, Symbols and Religious Objects

Holy shrine

Next to the Bodhi tree at Bodh Gaya is the magnificent Mahabodhi temple. It was built thousands of years ago and has always been an important place of pilgrimage for Buddhists. It is shaped like a pyramid and has very ornate carvings on the outside walls. Inside is a large statue of the Buddha that faces exactly towards the spot where the Buddha was Enlightened.

▶ The Mahabodhi temple is visited by thousands of pilgrims each year.

The Buddha's footprint

Near the city of Kandy in Sri Lanka is the mountain, Sri Pada. Buddhist pilgrims believe that the Buddha travelled there. At the top of the mountain is a stone marked with footprints. Buddhists believe that these were left by the Buddha.

WHAT DO YOU THINK?

Why do you think it is important for worshippers to visit holy places?

The Buddha's stupa

At Kushinagara in northern India, there is a stupa that was built at the place where the Buddha passed away. Pilgrims who visit walk around the stupa at least three times to remember the Buddha and his teachings. There is also a temple, called the Nirvana temple, and inside it is a huge statue of the Buddha. It is seven metres long.

▼ The statue at the temple in Kushinagara shows the Buddha lying down just before he passed away.

Glossary

Bodhi tree a large fig tree that grows in India. The Buddha gained Enlightenment under a Bodhi tree

Buddhists people who follow the teachings of the Buddha

burial mounds places where someone has been buried

chanting repeating the same words over and over again in a song-like way

cremated when the body of a dead person is burned instead of buried

Dharma Wheel the Buddha's teachings are called Dharma. The Dharma Wheel shows Buddhists how they can follow these teachings

Enlightenment understanding the truth about how life really is and how you can be happy

holy men men who spend all their time talking about religion and the meaning of life

incense a thin stick that is covered in perfumed material. It is lit at one end and as it burns, it fills the air with a sweet smell

meditate to sit quietly and clear the mind of all thoughts

monks holy men

Nirvana a Buddhist word meaning perfect peace and happiness

nuns holy women

pilgrims people who make a journey to a religious place of great importance

pilgrimages journies pilgrims make

puja an act of worship and respect

sacred something that is very important for religious reasons

shrine a special place used for worship

stupa a place where the ashes of the Buddha or other important Buddhists are buried

temples buildings for prayer and religious ceremonies

Quizzes

Try these questions to see how much you remember about Buddhism.

Are these facts true or false?

1. Buddhism began in India.
2. To meditate you clap and sing.
3. Buddhists take off their shoes when they enter the temple.
4. The Buddha gained Enlightenment under a palm tree.
5. One of the symbols of Buddhism is the lotus flower.

Which of these is the odd one out?

Answers are on the next page.

Index

Answers:

1 True

2 False, you sit quietly

3 True

4 False, it was a Bodhi tree, which is a type of fig tree

5 True

C is the odd one out. All the other objects are found in the shrine room

OUR PLACES OF WORSHIP

Contents of titles in the series:

WAYLAND